# Scenic Driving

# THE BEARTOOTH HIGHWAY

*Montana and Wyoming*

H. L. James

FALCON®

Creech
Gristmill

**ᴀFALCON**GUIDE®

© 1997 Falcon® Publishing, Inc.
Helena, Montana.

Editing, design, typesetting, and other prepress work by Falcon®, Helena, Montana.

Printed in the United States of America.

1 2 3 4 5 6 7 8 9 0 MG 03 02 01 00 99 98

**Library of Congress Cataloging-in-Publication Data**
James, H. L. (Harold L.), 1933-
    Scenic driving the Beartooth Highway : Montana and
Wyoming / H. L. James.
        p.   cm.
    Includes bibliographical references (p.   ).
    ISBN 1-56044-637-4 (pbk.)
    1. Beartooth Highway (Mont. and Wyo.) — Tours. 2. Automobile
travel — Beartooth Highway (Mont. and Wyo.) — Guidebooks. I. Title.
F737.B35J36   1997
917.86'6 — dc21                                97-11223
                                                  CIP

Excerpt on page iii from DATELINE AMERICA by Charles Kuralt, © 1979 by CBS, Inc., reprinted by permission of Harcourt Brace & Company.

Illustrative materials courtesy of the Montana Bureau of Mines and Geology.

Front cover photo by George Robbins.

Color section photos by Michael Sample.

For extra copies of this book please check with your local bookstore, or write Falcon®, P.O. Box 1718, Helena, MT 59624. You may also call toll-free 1-800-582-2665. To contact us via email, visit our web site at http: \\ www.falconguide.com.

*Na Pet Say*
—THE BEAR'S TOOTH

—RED LODGE, MONTANA. Alice Mitchell of Aberdeen, Washington, says she is planning a vacation trip with her family. She says in her letter to me, "You have been on the road for as long as I can remember. So tell me, what are America's most beautiful highways?"

All right, Mrs. Mitchell, here goes.

The most beautiful road in America is U.S. 212, which leaves Red Lodge, climbs to Beartooth Pass at eleven thousand feet, and drops down into the northeast entrance of Yellowstone Park. Don't try it in winter, Mrs. Mitchell; U.S. 212 spends the winter under many feet of snow. When the road opens, usually in May, the folks in Cooke City set up a booth to give the first day's intrepid motorists free drinks on the way through. It's that kind of highway. There will still be snow up there in August, but it's America's most beautiful road.

*—Charles Kuralt*

# THE
# BEARTOOTH AREA

◆

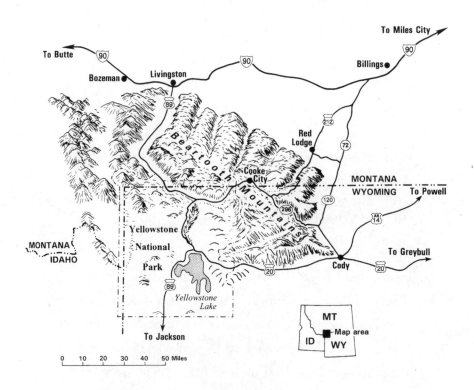

# CONTENTS

◆

# FOREWORD

◆

Welcome to a scenic *tour de force* — the Beartooth Highway. Few, if any, mountain roads in the United States can compare with it. It is the essence of a high-country excursion. Charles Kuralt called it "the most beautiful road in America." The 64-mile corridor offers spectacular scenery, varied topography, and examples of dramatic geologic processes. It is a vertical place, where the route literally crosses the "top" of both Montana and Wyoming. It is also an overwhelming place, and, as one stands on the summit of Beartooth Pass, it is difficult to comprehend all that took place here.

There are more than 25 features labeled "Beartooth": a lake, a butte, a creek, a waterfall, a pass, a canyon, and a plateau, just to name a few; there is even a "Beartooth burger"! The word comes from a conspicuous mountain spire the Crow Indians called *Na Pet Say* — the "bear's tooth."

Called "the Granites" in the early part of this century, the Beartooth Mountains — which include Granite Peak, the crown point of Montana (12,799 feet) — are part of the Absaroka-Beartooth Wilderness: a reserved region (904,500 acres) where humans are only visitors who quickly pass through. It was included in the Wilderness Act signed by President Jimmy Carter on March 27,

*Tourist promotion, circa 1939.* MONTANA HISTORICAL SOCIETY

1978. Additional recognition for the area came on February 8, 1989, when the Beartooth Highway joined 52 other routes to become a National Scenic Byway. Here, on-site travelers can view a diverse natural history that portrays a unique environmental picture of high aesthetic values.

Welcome to a scientific time laboratory where some of the oldest and youngest rocks on Earth are displayed in spectacular fashion. Welcome to a landscape of magnificent proportions. Welcome to alpine lakes, wildflower-carpeted meadows, lush forests, glacier-carved skylines, pristine streams, and magnificent vistas of bordering prairies on distant horizons. Welcome to a place with clean air and clear water. Welcome to the Beartooth Highway!

*"I always enjoy packing up there [Beartooths], because it may be as close to heaven as I will ever get."*
*—Clarks Fork outfitter, 1993*

# ACKNOWLEDGMENTS

◆

This book is a revised version of a technical publication entitled *Geologic and Historic Guide to the Beartooth Highway, Montana and Wyoming* released by the Montana Bureau of Mines and Geology in Butte in 1995. That original publication received the 1996 "Best Guidebook Award" presented by the Geoscience Information Society. Those readers who wish for a more detailed geologic story of the Beartooth Highway and its environs can consult that release, listed as Special Publication 110.

Unless otherwise credited, all illustrations, graphics, and sketch art, including photographs from the Montana Historical Society and the Flashmore Collection, were used with the permission of the Montana Bureau of Mines and Geology. The author is grateful to Tom Egenes of Red Lodge for providing access to the Flashmore Collection, and to Rebecca Kohl of the Montana Historical Society in Helena for her assistance. Grateful appreciation is also extended to Clint Dawson, Shoshone National Forest (Powell, WY), for furnishing aerial photographs. The attractive sketch art is from the pen of Diane Nugent of Kalispell.

DIANE NUGENT © 1986

# GEOLOGY

◆

The Beartooth Mountains form a northwest-trending uplift in south-central Montana and northwestern Wyoming. The massif is roughly 75 miles long and 40 miles wide, is nearly rectangular in shape, and rises abruptly and impressively 4,000 to 5,000 feet above the Crazy Mountain Basin on the north and the Bighorn Basin to the east. The mountains were formed during late Cretaceous and early Tertiary time (80-55 million years ago). During the course of the mountain building, the uplift penetrated thick covers of sedimentary rock. Throughout its rise, the sedimentary cover was "piggybacked" on the granitic rocks—as evidenced by remnants such as Beartooth Butte. The upheaval is divided into three units: the North Snowy block (Livingston area), the South Snowy block (Cooke City area), and the Beartooth block (Red Lodge area). The latter, popularly referred to as the Beartooth Plateau, is the largest and southeasternmost block, and is the part of the uplift crossed by the Beartooth Highway.

The Beartooth uplift, including all three blocks, is the highest upland in the middle Rocky Mountain region. It also contains the largest single exposure of Precambrian rocks in the region. Dated by geologists at 3.96 billion years, some Beartooth rock samples are considered parts of the oldest rocks on Earth.

The topography of the northern part of the Beartooth block is extremely rugged, consisting of intensely glaciated terrain with boulder-strewn mantles, jagged peaks, ice-gouged basins, and steep-walled canyons. Altitudes range from 5,500 feet along the lower Stillwater River to 12,799 feet at Granite Peak, the highest point in Montana. The southern and eastern parts are considerably less rugged; 2,000 feet lower in elevation, they are characterized by five distinct erosional surfaces named the Beartooth, Hell Roaring, Line Creek, Red Lodge Creek, and Silver Run plateaus. In no other alpine setting in the United States are such broad, high-altitude tablelands so well preserved and magnificently defined. The south-western sector of the block is also strikingly glaciated. Nearly 1,000 feet lower in elevation than the adjacent plateaus, it is character-ized by an extensive area of ice-carved basins holding numerous lakes. Also located in the southwest corner is a prominent, isolated relic, Beartooth Butte, which rises more than 1,600 feet above the surrounding ice-scoured tracts. The picturesque landmark, situated near the midway point on the Beartooth Highway, is an excellent example of a remnant of younger sedimentary rocks that previously existed on the uplift. The extreme southwestern bound-ary of the Beartooth block is sharply marked by the 3,000-foot-deep Clarks Fork Canyon.

The scenic grandeur of the present Beartooth Mountains is due principally to the action of glaciation. During the Pleistocene Epoch, which began about 1.6 million years ago, extensive ice fields covered a majority of the uplift, with only the highest topographic points projecting above the glacier blankets. In the eastern and southeastern sectors of the Beartooth block, parts of the original stripped Precambrian surface escaped glacial sculpting; these

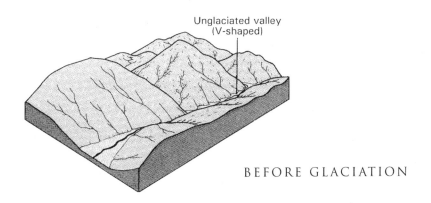

Unglaciated valley
(V-shaped)

BEFORE GLACIATION

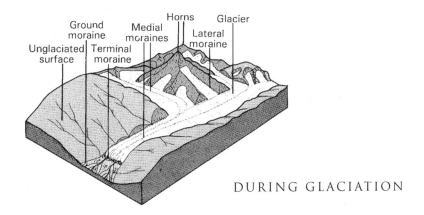

Ground
moraine

Medial
moraines

Horns

Glacier

Unglaciated
surface

Terminal
moraine

Lateral
moraine

DURING GLACIATION

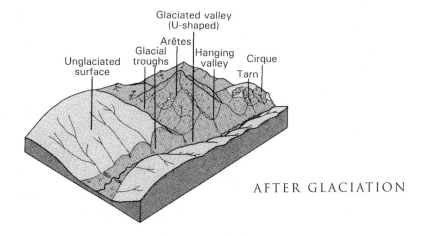

Glaciated valley
(U-shaped)

Arêtes

Glacial
troughs

Hanging
valley

Cirque

Unglaciated
surface

Tarn

AFTER GLACIATION

*Glacial stages of the Beartooth Mountains.*

areas apparently never accumulated enough snow to generate a gravity impetus sufficient to force ice movement. The effects of the Pleistocene climate are evident, however, in the frost-shattered surfaces characterized by accumulations of rock fields. Where glaciation was initiated along lines of pre-existing drainage (e.g., Rock Creek), the surface was sharply dissected, resulting in distinctive, separate, plateau-type benches that are unique to the character of the mountains. The alpine glaciation of the highlands ultimately transformed large parts of the surface into classic examples of excavated U-shaped troughs, hanging valleys, cirques, horns, rock basins, and arêtes that today provide the magnificent landscape. In the lower elevations, evidence of this great erosive power and transport is found in the form of moraines and glacial outwash plains.

The full record of Beartooth glaciation is far from complete. Only identifiable observations from the final two episodes, which concluded approximately 130,000 and 12,000 years ago, can be reconstructed with any degree of certainty. Furthermore, the glacial activity that provided the splendid scenery is no longer at work in the mountains. Undoubtedly, small, secluded ice patches still exist at the higher elevations, but few, if any, would extend beyond the shadow of their own cirques.

# HISTORY

◆

When a large-beaked bird soars on updrafts from a nearby canyon, the Crow Indians are reminded of their Sioux ancestry. In the Hidatsa tongue of the Sioux, they called themselves *Absarokee*, a combination of the words *Absa*, meaning a large-beaked bird (interpreted as the raven), and *Rokee*, referring to their children. In recorded history, the Beartooths and the neighboring Pryor Mountains became their adopted homeland, settled by migratory bands from the upper Midwest in the early 1600s.

But long before the "bird people" arrived, paleohumans intermittently occupied environs of the Beartooth Mountains starting in 10,000 B.C., as evidenced by some Clovis Period tools discovered on the flats east of Red Lodge. The survival of these early peoples hinged on big game: mastodon, mammoth, long-horned bison, and camel. During droughts of the Altithermal Period (7500–5000 B.C.), the uplands provided a more dependable supply of food and water where forays were rewarded with smaller game: deer, sheep, rabbits, and rodents. Deeply scoured river canyons and alpine lakes served as sources of fish.

For generations, people lived in scattered groups, but by 1100 A.D., a societal matrix began to emerge in North America, which included communal dwellings, planting of crops, development of basketry, pottery, and hunting implements, trading, and, of singular importance, the perfecting of the bow and arrow. As populations increased, political structures formed into tribes (i.e., Sioux, Cheyenne, Arapahoe, Crow, Shoshone-Bannock), and competition for food and territory intensified. Boundaries that separated the various bands were arbitrary, and probably most area residents frequented the Beartooth Mountains at various times during the summer months.

When the Spanish introduced the horse into the Southwest in the sixteenth century, lifestyles on the northern plains became mobile too, both in pursuit of game and in retaliation against warring factions. By the early 1800s, the buffalo herds in what is now eastern Idaho had been hunted almost to extinction. This led to the development of the Bannock Trail where large hunting migrations were made each spring across the Yellowstone Plateau to the headwaters of Soda Butte Creek, down the Clarks Fork of the Yellowstone, and out onto the eastern plains that lay between the Musselshell and Yellowstone rivers north of present-day Billings, Montana. The thoroughfare lasted in varying degrees well into the 1870s. It was eventually severed when the ever-increasing white population began to encroach into the region. In its final days, the eastern section of the trail served as an escape route for the fleeing Nez Perce tribe in the summer of 1877.

The first white men to see the Beartooth area were members of the Lewis and Clark Expedition, the Corps of Discovery. Returning from the Pacific Coast in the summer of 1806, William Clark and his party passed along the north face of the mountains as they descended the Yellowstone River. No explorations were made into side canyons at that time, because the group was hastening to rejoin Lewis at the confluence with the Missouri River. To one member of the Corps of Discovery, however, the region was intriguing enough to prompt a resignation from the homeward bound expedition. Downstream from the confluence, John Colter turned back, and from the mouth of the Bighorn River headed southwest in pursuit of the fur trade. As a mountain man and trapper, Colter embarked on a remarkable odyssey during the winter of 1807-8 into present-day Wyoming and eastern Idaho. His travels covered an incredible 500 miles, accomplished across rough terrain, on foot, alone, and without benefit of guides and interpreters. He was the first white man to report the thermal features in what is now Yellowstone National Park. A sketch map, which was later published by Clark in 1814, shows Colter's trail, but it is of such speculative geography that reconstructing the exact route of his wanderings is impossible because he did not keep a journal. However, some topographic delineations that can reasonably be identified would place him along the Clarks Fork, possibly traveling with a band of Indians on the Bannock Trail.

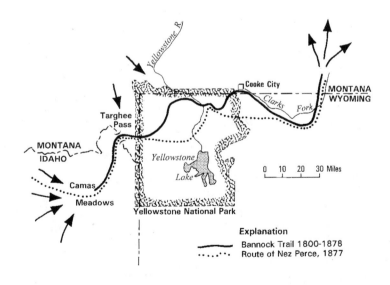

Bannock Trail, 1800-1878.

The stories that Colter brought out from the area were labeled pure fantasy, but they provided a rush of copy for reporters of the period: outlandish tales from this strange, unknown "corner of Louisiana" called Colter's Hell by the unbelieving. The 1820s ushered in the era of the fur trapper, and the likes of Osborne Russell and Jim Bridger. The "boiling cauldron" stories told at rendezvous brought the curious, and with them, a vindication for Colter.

Next came the gold seekers, as the territory of Montana began yielding its wealth in the early 1860s. This was followed by organized Yellowstone expeditions like the Folsom-Cook-Peterson party (1869), the Washburn-Langford-Doane effort (1870), and the Hayden Survey (1871). The latter ultimately persuaded the U.S. Congress to set aside the area as the first national park in the United States on March 1, 1872—the first such land reserve in history. Now tourism became a factor. Notwithstanding the absence of improvements, accommodations, and accessibility, five hundred people actually visited the new park during the first summer of its existence. Five years later, two tourists accidentally encountered the fleeing Nez Perce and were killed.

As conveyors of migrants and immigrants to the mineral grounds, railroads soon replaced the river steamers, and on September 8, 1883, the Northern Pacific had spanned the length of Montana. A "gold-en spike" ceremony at Gold Creek completed its transcontinental con-

### Hayden Survey, 1871

*Receiving an appropriation of $40,000, Ferdinand V. Hayden, leader of the newly created U.S. Geological and Geographical Survey of the Territories, set forth from Ogden, Utah on June 11, 1871, with a party of 35 men and 7 wagons to explore the Yellowstone region. The group included a young landscape painter, Thomas Moran, and an Omaha photographer named William Henry Jackson. The artistic renderings by these two individuals, coupled with the 500-page report by Hayden, persuaded legislators to set aside the area as the first national park in the United States on March 1, 1872.*

nection. Two south-central spurs from the mainline played significant roles in the development of the Beartooth region: the upper Yellowstone River route (completed in 1883) from Livingston south to Cinnabar brought tourists to the northern boundary of the park; and the Red Lodge route (completed in 1889) branched south from Laurel to service the newly discovered coal fields.

The railroads brought economic development to otherwise remote corners of Montana, when the lack of one could mean isolation. Cooke City's unsuccessful attempts to secure a line to the New World mining district in the 1880s have kept the community in a time warp; it remains much as it was during the latter part of the 19th century. This separation from the "outside world," many say, is part of the idyllic charm that continues to attract people to the undeveloped community.

In 1898, Cooke City briefly hosted the first scientific investigation of the Beartooth Mountains. Co-funded by the Rockefeller family and the Rocky Fork Coal Company, the expedition was led by geologist and mining engineer James Putnam Kimball. The party, outfitted in Bozeman in early July, consisted of eight men, including a Norwegian-born, Seattle-based photographer named Andres Wilse. The principal purpose of the field study was a mineral reconnaissance of the area that lay between the headwaters of the Clarks Fork and Stillwater drainages.

Reaching Cooke City on July 24, 1898, Kimball likened the hamlet to a Swiss village, noting that there were fewer than 100 inhabitants. He also observed: "A summer climate at high altitudes finer than that of Cooke would be difficult to find and a more attractive landscape hardly possible."

After traversing to the northeast (to the end of the wagon road at Kersey Lake), the group proceeded over pathless ground and established a series of base camps above timberline. These central-ized locations were interspersed with occasional "frosty bivouacs," including one at Goose Lake they labeled Camp Misery. Their un-dertaking was extremely arduous, and hazardous as well. The trans-fer of supplies, equipment, and pack animals over slick pavements of glacier-polished granite surfaces, and the precarious crossings over block fields, talus slopes, and deep chasms, were treacherous.

Inclement weather plagued the mission. Working at altitudes near 10,000 feet, the men experienced gale-force winds, snow, rain, hail, and freezing temperatures that severely hampered their ac-tivities, becoming at times a test of human endurance. Scaling the principal peaks to obtain astronomical readings was toilsome and time-consuming and placed some members in the predicament of making nighttime excursions back to camp, guided only by the bea-con of their distant campfire. A successful ascent of Granite Peak, Montana's highest projection, was denied the expedition, however. For unexplained reasons, the climb was aborted at an elevation of 11,447 feet—well below the 12,799-foot summit. (The first suc-cessful ascent of Granite Peak was accomplished by Billings moun-taineer Fred Inabnit in 1923. Mt. Inabnit [11,924 feet] near Rainbow Lake is named in honor of the Swiss-born immigrant.)

Having spent 102 strenuous days in the field—amazingly, without serious mishap—the expedition exited the mountains to the east via the Sheridan Trail. They pitched their final camp on Rocky Fork (Rock Creek) above Red Lodge. After several days of rest, the hardy contingent formally disbanded on October 11, 1898.

Although brief in terms of scientific interpretations and con-clusions, findings of the study did contribute significantly to the knowledge of previously uncharted terrain: "A mysterious *terra incognita*," Kimball called it in 1899. Many of the place names in the Beartooth Mountains are attributed to the expedition, as well as

*Members of the Kimball Expedition pose near the rugged northern crestline of the Beartooth Mountains, 1898.* MONTANA HISTORICAL SOCIETY

the first barometric recording of elevations.

In the 1920s, as roads improved and transportation graduated from horse-drawn coaches to automobiles, the curious filled the byways, particularly those heading to Yellowstone National Park. The pace soon quickened as cars began achieving the "dizzying speeds" of 25 miles per hour. The natural wonders and beauty

*Camp Sawtooth*, circa 1955. FLASHMORE COLLECTION

of the region were at times more than the eye could observe from a car, leading the noted conservationist John Muir to remark on tourism in general: "Nothing can be done well at a pace of forty miles a day."

A traveling public became a camping public, and with the change came a spirit of outdoor adventure. Along the main watercourses that drained the eastern and southern Beartooths, resorts, guest ranches, lodges, and hunting facilities sprang up. Places like Richel Lodge on Rock Creek, Camp Senia on the West Fork, and the L Bar T Ranch in the valley of the Clarks Fork became extremely popular tourist havens of the 1930s and 1940s. Two secluded, sought-after locations on the summit of the plateau—where guests had to be packed in—were Camp Sawtooth (1922-

*Richel Lodge, circa 1948.* FLASHMORE COLLECTION

*Campers in Yellowstone National Park, circa 1927.* NATIONAL PARK SERVICE

1962) along a meadow bordering Littlerock Creek, and Camp Beartooth (1933-1966) by the shores of Beartooth Lake. Neither of these facilities exists today. Only foundations and a chimney stack from the main building mark the site of Camp Sawtooth, while a USDA Forest Service campground at Beartooth Lake has obliterated all traces of Camp Beartooth.

In the modern era, tourism and recreation continue to be major contributors to the local economy, supplemented in part by small area ranches and irrigated farms. With the completion of the Beartooth Highway in 1936, a seasonal base of revenue was assured from the sightseeing motorist.

# BEARTOOTH EXPEDITION

## 1882

The first organized crossing of the Beartooth Plateau was accomplished in the summer of 1882 by an expedition party led by General Philip H. Sheridan. It was an unscheduled sojourn; the decision to cross the range—a feat deemed impossible—was made on the trail, an impromptu alternative that would cut three days of travel from the established Clarks Fork Yellowstone route. An ulterior motive may have been the challenge to cross a terrain where others had failed. At least twice before, U.S. Army detachments had tried unsuccessfully to conquer the impregnable Beartooths: Captain W. P. Clark's reconnaissance group of 1878, and the Montana-Wyoming boundary survey party of 1880.

The Beartooth "detour" came at the end of a summer inspection tour that General Sheridan, as Commander of the Division of the Missouri, had begun on August 7, 1882, at Green River, Wyoming. Following a visit to Fort Washakie, his group ascended the Wind River and crossed into the watersheds of the Gros Ventre Mountains via Lincoln Pass (present-day Sheridan Pass). Striking the Snake River along the Teton front, they turned north again and followed that stream into Yellowstone National Park.

By August 24, 1882, the group had made their way to the north end of the park, camping at Baronett Bridge over the Yellowstone River a few miles below the Lower Falls. The following morning they turned southeast and traveled up the Lamar drainage (calling it the "east fork" of the Yellowstone) to the mouth of Soda Butte Creek, and then up that tributary to a campsite approximately 11 miles downstream from Cooke City. Passing through the mining hamlet on August 26, the general reported on the value of the local mines, the courtesy of the inhabitants, and the number of town lots that were for sale. A short distance beyond, at what is now Colter Pass, he encountered a hunter named Geer who knew of a way across the Beartooths. Apparently impressed with Geer's knowledge and with the prospects of saving three days of travel, the general employed him to lead them across the mountains, somewhat against the judgment of others in the group.

They proceeded down the banks of the upper Clarks Fork, but a forest fire temporarily blocked their path. The group managed to make camp on the river beneath Pilot and Index peaks. As they began their ascent of the southwest flanks of the mountains the next morning, the general wrote: "Our trail over the Beartooth range was unmarked, and where trails were followed they were made by elk, bear, and deer." The next day's travel covered 13 miles, and a midday camp was made on the twenty-seventh below a prom-inent landmark referred to as "Red butte" (Beartooth Butte).

> *"Our trail over the Beartooth range was unmarked, and where trails were followed they were made by elk, bear, and deer."*
> —Gen. Philip H. Sheridan, 1882

Resuming march on August 28, they passed along the shores of what is now called Island Lake and ascended easterly across patchy snowfields to a summit where a grand panorama of the Bighorn and Pryor mountains presented itself. Descending a natural divide (Line Creek Plateau) that separated two streams that the general called "Big Rocky" (Rock Creek) and "Little Rocky" (Line Creek), the expedition made its way to the edge of the plateau. The final Beartooth camp was pitched at the base of the mountains in the narrow valley of Line Creek following a precipitous descent where the only mishap was a pack mule falling from the trail. Fortunately, the animal was rescued after it landed in the top of a pine tree.

On August 29, the party traversed a fatiguing section of badlands along the western perimeter of the Clarks Fork valley. They made camp ten miles above Bridger crossing. Continuing down the fertile valley to its mouth at the Yellowstone River and then heading east, the general and his command arrived in Billings at 1:00 P.M. on August 31, 1882. After a few hours spent transferring equipment and supplies, they departed for Chicago on the Northern Pacific Railroad at eight o'clock the same evening.

The tour took three weeks and covered approximately 600 miles. The party consisted of 12 officers, 56 enlisted men, and 61 assorted attachés (guides, packers, hunters, stewards, blacksmiths, etc.). The 129-member caravan traveled on 104 horses and 157 mules, averaging a little over 28.5 miles a day.

The unofficial Beartooth Expedition did accomplish a mission, however vague and unintentional its original purpose might have been. The general hailed it as "triumphantly successful in succeeding where others were turned back." The fact of achieving access, at least with pack animals, certainly qualifies Sheridan's effort as the forerunner of today's modern route. Observations made on the expedition prompted General Sheridan to offer several suggestions to his government. He proposed that Yellowstone National

Park be extended 40 miles to the east and 10 miles to the south to take advantage of the scenic values of the Beartooth Mountains. Although no action was ever taken on this proposal, it did lead to the establishment nine years later of forest reserves that encompass the range.

[*The following excerpt of General Sheridan's report dealing with the Beartooth section of the expedition is reprinted from Senate Report No. 911, Serial No. 2087, the 47th Congress (2nd Session): Government Printing Office, Washington D.C.*]

## BEARTOOTH REPORT, 1882

*by General Philip H. Sheridan*

The next morning our direction was up the east fork until we reached the mouth of Soda Butte creek, thence up that creek until we found a beautiful place for our camp, distant from Cooke City about 11 miles. The country passed over this day's march I think may fairly be considered the best grass and the best wintering country inside of the national park. There are rich bottom lands, surrounded by bald, grassy mountains, dotted with groves of timber, principally of the different varieties of the pine family and the quaking aspen.

August 26, resumed the march, passing through Cooke City, a mining town on the divide between the waters of the east fork of the Yellowstone River and Clark's Fork. Many of the mines here are considered valuable. There are about 100 houses in the city, with fair prospects of as many more in a few months, indicated by the quantities of freshly hewn logs lying about and the number of town lots for sale. After stopping for only a short time to make some inquiries of the courteous inhabitants we continued on our way.

Just as we reached the summit of the divide, where the waters of Soda Butte Creek and Clark's Fork take their respective watersheds, we met a hunter, Mr. Geer, who considered himself so familiar with the Beartooth range of mountains that I was induced to abandon the old Clark's Fork trail and make an effort to cross that range, thus saving about three days in our journey to Billings station on the Pacific railroad.

After meeting him and employing him as a guide, somewhat against the judgment of older guides, we passed down the mountain with much difficulty, on account of the burning forests, the fire extending across our line of march. The journey this day was through high mountain peaks, covered on top with perpetual snow. We encamped at the base of Index peak and Pilot knob, on the banks of Clark's Fork of the Yellowstone. This camp was named Camp Clark, after Captain W. P. Clark, second cavalry, our Indian interpreter. Distance marched, 31 miles; altitude of camp, 7,100 feet.

In the evening, just before dinner, the hunters who had gone off the day before on our left flank, over in the direction of Hell Roaring creek, returned with buffalo, elk, deer and antelope. They saw a herd of about 140 buffalo and killed four.

On the morning of August 27, under the direction of our new guide, we crossed to the north side of Clark's Fork and began the ascent of the Beartooth Range. This was long, but gradual, and quite feasible for a wagon road so far as grade is concerned. The only difficulties which presented themselves during the day were bodies of densely growing timber at one or two places. However, we got through these without much delay, and about 12 o'clock encamped immediately under a very prominent land mark, called on the map Red butte. The camp was beautiful and was named Camp Gregory, after Colonel Gregory of my staff.

The country traveled over was open and grassy, bunch and gama grasses predominating. Distance marched, 13 miles; altitude of camp, 9,400 feet. From our camp this day we were high enough to obtain a complete view of the whole Rocky mountain range for several hundred miles, with its snowcapped peaks and massive beds of snow, drifted in places to a depth of 40 to 50 feet in the craters and summit ravines. Several lakes, large and small, were in plain view beneath us on the lower levels.

Next day, August 28, we resumed our march at 6:16 A.M., passing along the border of one of these summit lakes, very deep and a mile and a half or two miles in diameter. The edge of the lake, having a small margin of mud, was very much tracked up by grizzly bear, elk and deer. We continued eastward, still ascending, and crossed numerous beds of perpetual snow, solid enough to permit our horses and pack train to traverse them without breaking through. At about 11 A.M. we reached the summit level of our trail. We were here far above the timber line, and although our pathway was covered with spring flowers, the grasses were coarse and unnutritious. The view to the eastward gave us the high, snowclad range of the Big Horn mountains with Pryor's mountain range lying intermediate. The view from this high altitude was grand, extending in every direction to the limit of vision with good field glasses. We had now reached the headwaters of the Little and Big Rocky, streams that enter into the main fork of Clark's river, well down toward its mouth.

Our progress was down a natural divide between Little and Big Rocky, until we arrived at the edge of the canyon, whence there was an abrupt descent to the plain below, distant from us about nine miles. At first I thought of sending the escort ahead to break and remove obstructions from the trail but soon discovered that the men would consume too much time in trying to make too good a trail; that it was best to take the advance down the mountain and let the escort follow.

We all got down safely; one mule only fell from the trail and caught in the top of a tree growing up from a point below. Unharmed, and with his pack on, we cut him out of the tree on the side of the mountain, without further accident reaching our camp in the valley of the Little Rocky at the base of the Range.

We had to walk most of the distance down the declivity, but our riding horses and pack train came down the mountain without inconvenience or accident, excepting the mule which fell off the trail, as before described. Notwithstanding that mishap, I am satisfied that a well-packed mule can go either up or down where a horse can be led. Distance marched, 25 miles; altitude of camp, 5,890 feet. This camp was named Camp Wheelan, after Capt. J. N. Wheelan,

Second cavalry, commanding our escort.

Considering that it was the latter part of August, the fact that the country traveled over most of the day was covered here and there with deep snow, coarse grasses and early spring flowers, indicated high altitudes and difficulty in crossing on this trail until late in the summer season. On passing a beautiful little mountain lake with beds of snow near it, the head of the column came suddenly upon a drove of about 200 elk, and, as the hunters had all gone out on the flanks of the column, not a gun was at hand. Although this large drove of magnificent animals turned around when they discovered us, and for a moment ran toward the head of the column, no one was ready but Geer, the guide, who, after some delay in getting his gun out of its case, got a shot which killed a fine doe. The men of the escort farther in the rear opened quite a fusillade but the game was too far off.

The hunters came in that evening with only one elk, although if they had been at the head of the column they could have had as many as we might have desired to kill.

After a march of 25 miles we had crossed the Beartooth mountains and encamped on Little Rocky, whose valley was not especially large or prepossessing, but the clear, mountain stream contained thousands of brook trout. We had no time to pick our steps, but one who will do so will be able, in my opinion, to get a good, practicable trail for packing. By this trail the distance from the mouth of the Clark's Fork to Cooke City will be three days shorter than by the old Clark's Fork trail, and

I believe that it can be made, if it is not now, a better trail than the other.

On August 29, we resumed the march at 6:15 A.M., and I wish to say here, that in mentioning that we started at 6:15, which was the latest moment at which we started upon any morning during our journey, I mean that the whole command was ready and the mules packed at that time each morning.

In this day's march I gave way to the guides. I should have gone by the most direct line on our general course to the Big Rocky, and then Clark's Fork, but made the mistake of going directly east instead, expecting to strike the Clark's Fork about where the old Bridge road crosses that stream. The direction taken carried us at first over a good, grassy country, but it eventually led us into the badlands, so that we struck Clark's Fork at least 10 miles above the Bridger crossing and encamped there, after a march which I considered one of the most fatiguing of the entire trip. Distance traveled, 21 miles; altitude, 3,850 feet.

On the morning of August 30 we crossed Clark's Fork a little above our camp, proceeded down the valley, crossed the river again to the west bank at the Bridger ford, and continued our march until we crossed the Big Rocky. The valley of Clark's Fork opened out until, at places, it was five or six miles broad, the soil good, and bunch and gama grasses fine. We met, during the day, many of the Crow Indians, painted, and mounted on tough little ponies. Near our camp was a small village containing a number of women and children who were out gathering berries and wild plums.

On August 31, at 6:15 A.M. continued our march down the prolongation of the beautiful valley through which we marched yesterday. It opened out to the width of about eight miles as we approached the Yellowstone river, which we crossed by a very good ford just about the mouth of Clark's Fork.

We then continued down the north bank of the Yellowstone River to Billings station on the Northern Pacific railroad, arriving there about 1 P.M.

# BEARTOOTH CONSTRUCTION

## 1932–1936

As late as the mid-1800s, the environs of the Beartooth Mountains were known only to a few white men: trappers, guides, and hunters—the likes of George Geer and Red Lodge eccentric Ed VanDyke, who brought their game out along trails that they had marked. No established, usable pathway existed, and organized travel across the seemingly impassable canyons, rocks, and crags was strictly reserved for the hardy (or foolhardy). The Beartooth Expedition of 1882 proved that at least the southern part of the obstacle could be safely crossed, and that such a crossing could shorten the travel time between Cooke City and Red Lodge by three days.

Shortly after the turn of the century, various citizen groups began promotions to effect an improved route "across the top." Headed by an enthusiastic Red Lodge physician turned politician, John C. Siegfriedt, the group focused tirelessly on the tourism benefits of a scenic eastern approach to Yellowstone National Park. Their efforts were joined, in part, by concerned mining interests at

Cooke City, as the National Park Service threatened to stop commercial trucking of New World ore over park roads to the railhead at Gardiner. Supported by contributions and fund-raising activities, the group's first endeavor was a reconnaissance location survey, conducted in the summer of 1919 along the east side of Mt. Maurice, for a route that would reach the summit on Line Creek Plateau. This proposed route, called the Black and White Trail (from Forest Service maps), proved lengthy and unfeasible and was later abandoned for the present Rock Creek location.

As early as 1922, entrepreneurs began developing tourist camps along the scenic valley floor of Rock Creek. This brought improved roads that ultimately led into midsections of the canyon, thus making the Rock Creek approach shorter and more attractive for promotion purposes.

Following several years of lobbying disappointments, the biggest boost finally came in late 1925 when the Black and White Trail Association enlisted the support of Montana congressman Scott Leavitt. A former forester, Leavitt recognized the tourist potential of such a road; he championed the proposal by attaching the Beartooth Highway route as an amendment to his sponsored U.S. Congress legislation called the Park Approach Act (H.R. #12404). In essence, the act provided for construction and improvement of roads that led to national parks, which in turn would encourage and promote tourism. Final fruition came on January 31, 1931, when the Leavitt Bill was signed by President Herbert Hoover.

Funding for the highway was approved at $2,500,000, using monies from the Forest Service, from Federal Aid, and from allocated funds authorized by the Park Approach Act. The road's design and construction was under the auspices of the U.S. Bureau of Public Roads (the equivalent of the present-day Federal Highway Administration). Surveying and location studies of the route, which

*Dignitaries and officials at "first shovelful" ceremonies near mouth of Quad Creek, August 20, 1931.* FLASHMORE COLLECTION

began at Quad Creek (14 miles southwest of Red Lodge), were started almost immediately. Construction contracts were let on June 27, 1931, and partial construction began later that summer.

The successful bidders: Morrison Knudsen Company (Boise, Idaho) was awarded the switchbacks section from Quad Creek to the Wyoming border; McNutt and Pyle, Inc. (Eugene, Oregon) was granted the summit section from the state line to a point near the L Bar T Ranch in the Clarks Fork valley; and Winston Brothers Company (Minneapolis, Minnesota) submitted the low bid for the western part from the Clarks Fork valley through Cooke City to the northeast entrance to Yellowstone National Park. S. J. Groves

*Construction workers on lunch break, 1935.* FLASHMORE COLLECTION

& Sons (Minneapolis, Minnesota) was low bidder for the surfacing contract for the entire route. Other subcontractors on various phases included Utah Construction, Inc., and Collison & Dollivon Company. The Civilian Conservation Corps (CCC) was commissioned for specialized tasks, such as construction of hand-chiseled granite abutments for bridge crossings.

Each contractor had its own construction camp that housed workers, families, and equipment during the construction season. Morrison Knudsen built its tent camp along Rock Creek at the base of the switchbacks, and still lends its initials to the site where the Forest Service M-K Campground exists today. The McNutt and Pyle community was at Long Lake, where frame shacks lined the shore; these required reconstruction each spring after being flattened by winter snows. The Winston Brothers assembly was scattered between Cooke Pass (Colter Pass) and Cooke City.

The majority of the highway was built between 1932 and 1936 under chief engineer Charles B. Peterson. Considering terrain requirements, short seasonal construction periods, and weather, it was remarkable that the project was completed on time and within budget. It did, however, cost the lives of two workers. The engineering aspect of parts of the route, even by today's standards, is nothing short of phenomenal. For example, the 4,000-foot climb out of Rock Creek Canyon (7.5 miles at a grade exceeding 6 percent) on a sidehill slope that averages 30 degrees is "seat-of-your-pants" engineering at its best. A certain element of pride and accomplishment was generated during the building of the road, and rightfully so. Grateful workers, employed during the Great Depression, were productive workers, and this no doubt contributed to completing the herculean task on time.

Most names given to geographic points on the highway have not survived on current maps, but definitely represented some meaningful interpretation to workers at the time: "Primal Point," "Lunch Meadow," "High Lonesome Ridge," "Grizzly Knob," "Frozen Man's Curve," and "Inspiration Point," to name a few. Rock Creek Vista was known as "Knox Point" during construction days, and along nearby Wyoming Creek Canyon, a curving switchback carried the label "Mae West Curve" after a movie star of the era.

Although drivable for several days prior to its formal opening, the highway was officially dedicated on June 14, 1936, by a honking caravan. Two days later, the *Red Lodge Picket Journal* reported: "The Red Lodge–Cooke City–Yellowstone Park highway, declared impossible by many engineers, is today a reality."

# ROAD LOG

◆

## Red Lodge to Cooke City

The 64-mile road log is divided into three parts: Part I - Rock Creek Canyon (22 mi.), Part II - Beartooth Plateau (27 mi.), and Part III - Clarks Fork valley, which includes a short section along Soda Butte Creek at the west terminus (15 mi.).

The log was designed for reading from east to west. This course direction provides a more dramatic view of the principal features. Furthermore, driving east to west during morning hours will allow the user to take advantage of photographic lighting. During early spring and late fall, it is advisable to inquire about weather conditions: sudden, intense snowstorms are not uncommon at the higher elevations. Depending on weather, traffic, road conditions, and stops at points of interest, the drive usually requires about three hours (one-way).

The two-lane Beartooth Highway is generally open from late May to early October. Although paved throughout its length, the road is rough surfaced in some places, quite narrow in many places, without parking shoulders in most places, and rarely maintains a straight course at any place! The route is designed for slow to

*Beartooth Pass, 1937.* MONTANA HISTORICAL SOCIETY

moderate speeds. To maximize the enjoyment of a splendid high-country excursion, **drive carefully**. A $1.6 million construction project completed during the summer of 1994 has greatly improved the section between the switchbacks and the Wyoming border. A concurrent $750,000 expansion of the Rock Creek Vista area has attractively upgraded that facility.

*Rocky Fork coal mines at Red Lodge, 1896.* MONTANA HISTORICAL SOCIETY

For those who are not familiar with the use of a road log, the clock method is employed to direct the reader to specific sights. As you are driving, the front of the car is **always** at 12:00, and locations are referred to as if on the face of a clock; for example, 9:00 is 90 degrees left and 3:00 is 90 degrees right. Some calibrations in mileage may be required if detours are taken at recommended stops. Also, keep in mind that odometer readings will vary with vehicles and tire sizes from those listed in this log. Most of the illustrations are keyed to milepoints.

**PART I** ROCK CREEK CANYON

Located 3 miles downstream from the mouth of Rock Creek Canyon, the picturesque town of Red Lodge has a colorful Western past. Named for the painted lodges at a favored summer camp of the Crow Indians, the town (originally called Rocky Fork) was established as a stage stop on the Billings to Meeteetse (Wyoming) road in early 1883. On December 9, 1884, a post office was granted to the settlement, then located in Gallatin County. It was named the county seat of Carbon County in March 1895.

Coal was discovered in the mid-1880s, and the forming of the Rocky Fork Coal Company in 1887 resulted in a rush of European immigrants to the area—mostly Slavs. After the turn of the century, the company employed over 1,600 miners and maintained a steady production rate of one million tons of coal annually. By the early 1920s, the population had grown to 5,000. Prosperity was short lived, however, as the Great Depression, mine disasters, and the availability of less expensive strip-mined coal in southeastern Montana soon took their toll. By the late 1940s, commercial coal mining was nonexistent in the area. Since that time, the town has successfully recovered and maintains a robust year-round tourist industry. Many buildings and homes in Red Lodge are listed in the National Register of Historic Places, a fact which attests to the significance of the town's founding days. Annual events include the Mountain Man Rendezvous (July), the Home of Champions Rodeo (July), and Festival of Nations Celebration (August). Nearby Red Lodge Mountain receives over 250 inches of snow annually, and provides skiing from December to April.

# *Beginning of road log*

| Miles | Description |
|---|---|

**0.0** Mileage begins at junction of U.S. Highway 212 and Montana Highway 308, near the south city limits of Red Lodge (elev. 5,254 ft.).

MT 308 leads east to the ghost town of Washoe (3 mi.) and to the "almost" ghost town of Bearcreek, 4 miles beyond. Strung out along the sage-covered banks of Bear Creek, the two towns combined for a peak population of 7,000 in 1920. The Bearcreek coal field is an eastward extension of the Red Lodge field. In 1922, seven mines operated in the area, and overall they produced greater tonnage than the Red Lodge field. One of Montana's great mine disasters occurred in the Bear Creek field on February 27, 1943, when an explosion at the Smith No. 3 killed 74 men. The Bearcreek Saloon, an area-noted "watering hole" and home to occasional championship pig races and indoor iguana races, is the only business left in town.

**0.1** **Proceed southwesterly** on US 212 along the narrow flood plain of Rock Creek.

**0.3** Road to Red Lodge Mountain ski area to right.

**0.4** Old Meeteetse stage road to left.

**0.5** USDA Forest Service (Beartooth Ranger District), Custer National Forest offices on right can provide information on route and weather conditions.

**1.5** Bridge across West Fork of Rock Creek. Note boulder-strewn flood plain indicating past flood stages.

**1.6** Towne Point (elev. 7,966 ft.) at 1:00. White-colored rocks along mountain front at 1:00 are composed of vertical beds of limestone. The scenic area is locally known as the Palisades.

**1.8** The sparse vegetation cover (mainly sagebrush) on the surrounding hills is due principally to a lack of nutrients in the subsoil and to the porous

| Miles | Description |
| --- | --- |

nature of the soil, resulting in its inability to retain moisture.

**2.7** Note vertical hedgerows on lower slopes of Mt. Maurice at 10:00. The vegetation (Russian olive) was purposely planted in 1964 to retain snow on wind-susceptible slopes for the proposed Sundance ski area. Unfortunately, the idea failed—so did Sundance!

**3.4** Entering the mouth of Rock Creek Canyon. The flanking canyon walls are comprised of Precambrian granite and include some of the oldest rocks on Earth *(see Geology , pp. 1-2)*.

**3.6** Piney Dell area; side road on left leads to Yellowstone Bighorn Research Association (YBRA) camp. Conceived in 1930 as the "Red Lodge Project" by Professor W. Taylor Thom Jr. of Princeton University, YBRA was established to train students in field geology, and to serve as a base of operations for geological research and educational programs. Through contributions, local promotions, and grants, the station was located at two previous sites—Piney Dell (1931-1932) and Camp Senia on the West Fork of Rock Creek (1933-1935)—before land was acquired in 1936 to construct the present facility high on the north slopes of Mt. Maurice. The center is recognized as one of the leading scientific stations of its type in the nation. The two-session (30-35 attendees each) programs run from early June through August and attract students from throughout the United States as well as some foreign countries. Instruction is provided mainly by faculty members from Princeton, Amherst, and Franklin and Marshall universities.

**4.3** Road on left leads to east side of Rock Creek and to Sheridan and Ratine campgrounds. The loop access rejoins the highway at milepoint 7.4.

**4.8** Rock Creek Resort on left.

**5.6** Mouth of Sheridan Creek at 9:00. Named for General Philip H. Sheridan, who crossed the Beartooth Plateau in the summer of 1882, the creek was thought by some historians to have been the expedition's descent path from the summit; however, interpretation of the general's diary notes indicate that the party actually descended Line Creek (5 mi. south), calling it "Little Rocky" *(see Beartooth Expedition, p. 17)* . Sheridan Point (elev. 9,500 ft.) at 10:00.

*Bridge across Rock Creek below Black Pyramid Mountain, 1939.* FLASHMORE COLLECTION

| Miles | Description |
|-------|-------------|

*7.4*    Ratine and Sheridan campgrounds access on left. Westminster Spires on skyline at 12:00.

*7.5*    Entering Custer National Forest. The Beartooth Highway passes through Custer and Gallatin national forests in Montana and Shoshone National Forest in Wyoming.

Most of the maintenance of the Beartooth Highway is conducted by the National Park Service, which operates independently of the USDA Forest Service, and is headquartered at Yellowstone National Park. The Park Service has an easement for 200 feet on either side of the centerline of the highway. The Montana Highway Department is responsible for the section between Red Lodge and the Wyoming state line.

*West view (upstream) of Rock Creek Canyon near milepoint 9.3. Black Pyramid Mountain is on the right.* MONTANA HISTORICAL SOCIETY

| Miles | Description |
| --- | --- |
| 9.2 | Bridge across Rock Creek. The drainage was originally called Rocky Fork; General Sheridan referred to it as "Big Rocky." |
| 9.3 | Highway curves left. Black Pyramid Mountain (elev. 8,608 ft.) at 12:00. Lake Fork Canyon at 1:00 is a major glacier-carved tributary of Rock Creek. |
| 9.8 | Lake Fork Canyon road on right. The confluence of Lake Fork and Rock Creek (in the clearing partly visible through trees on the right) was the site of Richel Lodge *(see History, p. 12-13)*. Built in 1921, it was a popular guest resort that featured a log lodge (complete with its own waterwheel for generating electricity) and 13 cabins. After fire destroyed the main facility on September 11, 1966, the remaining structures were razed. |

*11.4*     Rock Creek Canyon road on right provides access to camping areas and to the summit of Hell Roaring Plateau at 1:00. Traces of the road can occasionally be seen high on the opposite canyon walls to the right. The road leads to chromite deposits that were open-pit mined on the plateau by U.S. Vanadium Corporation between 1942 and 1945. The ore was trucked to a concentration mill at Red Lodge.

*11.5*     Route leaves valley floor of Rock Creek and begins a gradual ascent of the east wall of the canyon.

*11.8*     Note coalescing avalanche chutes across canyon at 2:00 and small glacial cirque to the right.

*12.3*     Route passes through weather-closure gates at Wyoming Creek.

*13.9*     Impressive view ahead of classic U-shaped, glaciated Rock Creek Canyon *(see Geology, p. 4)*.

*14.1*     Quad Creek turnout on left. The narrow cleft of Quad Creek is crossed four times on the impending switchbacks.

*14.4*     **Caution (sharp curve)**; begin 7.5 miles of a remarkably engineered and constructed section of the Beartooth Highway *(see Beartooth Construction, p. 29)*. During the climb to the top of the Beartooth Plateau, travelers will negotiate 5 major switchbacks and gain nearly 4,000 feet in elevation .

*15.7*     Grouted backslope—one of several areas on the switchbacks that was treated to curtail troublesome rockfalls and backslope failures.

*17.5*     Switchback constructed around base of large cirque. The massive rock moraine is now being supplemented by rockfalls from avalanche chutes along the headwall of the cirque.

(ABOVE) *A rosy sunrise illuminates the Beartooth Mountains.*

(LEFT) *Hardy mountain buttercups along the Beartooth Highway.*

(TOP) *Marsh marigolds are often the first sign of spring along the Beartooth Highway.*
(BOTTOM) *Take the bridge over the "Big Rocky," Rock Creek, at mile 9.2.*

(TOP) *Glacier Lake at dawn.*
(BOTTOM) *Mt. Rearguard can be seen from mile 29.6 along the Beartooth Highway.*

(TOP) *Mile 37.4 marks a marvelous view of red-stained Beartooth Butte.*
(BOTTOM) *A bull moose wades in the shallows of an alpine lake.*

(TOP) *Look for the Bear's Tooth on the skyline at mile 27.5.*
(BOTTOM) *Snowmelt and spring rains feed this charming cascade flowing at the road's side.*

(ABOVE) *Clusters of arrowleaf balsamroot fill a Beartooth mountain meadow.*

(RIGHT) *Autumn aspen below Index and Pilot peaks. The peaks can be seen from recommended stop 7 at mile 43.2 along the Beartooth Highway.*

(ABOVE) *A serene alpine lake in a glacier-scoured landscape.*

(LEFT) *The landscape of the Beartooth Plateau is prime summer habitat for most Rocky Mountain fauna, including Rocky Mountain goats.*

(ABOVE) *The moon concludes its watch over the Beartooths.*

(RIGHT) *One of the many species of wildflowers to be found in the Beartooths, these purple pasque flowers seem lit from within.*

*Dramatic view of glacier-scoured upper Rock Creek Canyon.*
MONTANA TOURIST AND TRAVEL BUREAU

*Switchbacks on U.S. Highway 212 along the east wall of Rock Creek Canyon.*

| Miles | Description |
|-------|-------------|

**19.7**    **Recommended Stop 1:** Rock Creek Vista parking area on left (elev. 9,910 ft.). A short walk to a promontory provides a spectacular panorama along the entire course of Rock Creek Canyon, as well as of the adjoining deep cleft of Wyoming Creek. Across the canyon, the barren upland surface of Hell Roaring and Silver Run plateaus is also visible.

**19.9**    Weather-closure gates. Highway now extends for a short distance along the west wall of Wyoming Creek. Line Creek Plateau, on the horizon across the canyon to the east, is a frequent habitat for Rocky Mountain goats. Construction workers during the 1930s labeled this section of the roadway "Mae West Curve" *(see Beartooth Construction, p. 29).*

**20.7**    Small turnout on right for excellent view of Hell Roaring Plateau across Rock Creek Canyon.

**21.9**    Turnout on right near top of the Beartooth Plateau.

## PART II  BEARTOOTH PLATEAU

Welcome to the central theme of the presentation—the Beartooth Plateau. Here, the elevation is more than 10,000 feet above sea level. It is estimated that at this height, human lungs receive 15 percent less oxygen. Understandably, this requires a slower pace of activity. Weather conditions are rigorous and blizzards are frequent. Temperatures are near zero all winter and may drop below freezing on some mid-summer nights. High-velocity winds approaching 100 miles per hour can occur at any time. The average temperature is 26° F. Only the hardy survive here!

Travel across the upper surface of the plateau (approximately 20 mi.) can generally be regarded as an Arctic experience. Here is a landscape above timberline where only tundra, sedges, and small perennial flowering plants survive on shallow profiles of soil. For the most part, alpine glaciers shaped the mountainous terrain; they excavated the upland surfaces into deep canyons and depressions that today are represented by hundreds of lakes, ponds, and depressions. The climate still exerts the greatest influence on the present landscape: through alternating freezing and thawing. It continues to attack and break down the rock, causing further decomposition into a soil that ultimately washes away.

The summer fauna community includes most species found throughout the northern Rocky Mountains (Bighorn sheep, Rocky Mountain goats, elk, moose, mule deer, black bear, grizzly bear, coyote, and beaver), and most migrate downslope with the coming of winter. Only a few types of rodents, like the tiny pika, are permanent residents and remain active in the rock crevices beneath the snow cover. The fight for survival on the plateau is usually played out in a simplistic manner, and the food chain can be quite short; tundra plants are food for the pika, and the pika is food for the hawk.

| Miles | Description |
| --- | --- |
| 22.0 | The highway continues to ascend the barren, tundra-carpeted plateau. The rolling upper surface is occasionally interspersed by large block fields of granite. |
| 22.2 | Long curve to left. Ice-excavated trench at 2:00 is the headwaters of Quad Creek. |
| 22.8 | Canyon of Wyoming Creek on left; Line Creek Plateau on horizon at 9:00. |
| 23.5 | Road on left leads to Highline Creek trailhead parking. |
| 23.9 | Entering Park County, Wyoming and Shoshone National Forest. |
| 24.1 | Turnout on right at boundary of Shoshone National Forest. Originally called the Yellowstone Park Timberland Reserve, this was the first national forest in the United States. President Benjamin Harrison created it on March 30, 1891, in the first act of its kind to protect timber. With 2,431,914 acres, the Shoshone is the largest national forest in the Rocky Mountains. |
| 24.2 | Weather-closure gates. |

*Aerial view of Twin Lakes double cirque reveals the awesome excavating force of glacier ice. U.S. Highway 212 at upper left is in the vicinity of milepoint 25.3.*
SHOSHONE NATIONAL FOREST

| Miles | Description |
| --- | --- |

*25.3*    A series of small turnouts ahead on right provide excellent views of the Twin Lakes area.

*27.0*    **Recommended Stop 2:** Twin Lakes parking area. Twin Lakes is a large double cirque culminating in a hanging valley above Rock Creek Canyon. The ski tow on the cirque headwall is on a 60 degree slope (experts only!). The run is host to the annual Red Lodge International Summer Ski Racing Camp that trains world-class hopefuls.

*The Bear's Tooth.*

| Miles | Description |
| --- | --- |

**27.3** Small turnout on right. On a clear day, a partial view of the Bighorn Basin can be seen on the far left horizon. The double-peaked protrusion in the middle distance at 10:00 is Heart Mountain, which is located 15 miles north of Cody, Wyoming. Picturesque Littlerock Creek valley ahead on the left.

**27.5** Bear's Tooth (glacier-carved spire) on distant skyline at 12:00.

**28.2** Gardner Lake trailhead turnout on left. The lake occupies a cirque basin that is drained by Littlerock Creek. The creek is one of the principal streams that drains the eastern summits of the plateau; it provides irrigation water for area farms and ranches in the lowlands of the Bighorn Basin. Five miles downstream from the lake is the site of Camp Sawtooth, the first hunting facility in the eastern Beartooths *(see History, pp. 12, 14).* Deep Lake, 3 miles beyond, was formed by a large landslide which has blocked Littlerock Creek.

29.6    Turnout on right for view of the Bear's Tooth at 4:00. Mt. Rearguard to left (elev. 12,204 ft.).

29.9    Good view of upper reaches of ice-excavated Rock Creek Canyon on right.

30.5    **Recommended Stop 3:** Beartooth Pass (elev. 10,947 ft.) is the highest highway pass in Wyoming. Road on right leads to viewpoint and West Summit rest area, which offers a beautiful view of the Absaroka Range to the west. This location also provides an impressive view of a rugged "land of lakes" surface—ice sculpting at its best. From no other vantage point on the route is the excavating force of glaciers more evident.

30.9    Horseshoe Bend scenic area ahead provides a final view of the upper part of Rock Creek Canyon on right. Highway construction workers called this switchback "Frozen Man's Curve."

31.6    Curve; small turnout on right provides an excellent view of red-stained Beartooth Butte to the northwest, backdropped by Pilot Peak (left) and Index Peak on distant horizon at 2:30.

32.0    This location marks the **halfway point** between Red Lodge and Cooke City.

33.2    Small turnout on right above Frozen Lake. The route now enters an intensely glaciated area of the Beartooth Plateau.

*Beartooth Butte—a sedimentary island in a sea of granite.*

*33.6*  Highway passes through a stunted forest of white-bark pine and alpine fir. Survival of trees at this elevation is remarkable and a constant struggle. Wind abrasion, combined with deep blankets of winter snow, fashions trees into grotesque forms that resemble plantings by bonsai gardeners. *Krummholz*, a German word meaning crooked wood, is a term applied to this type of vegetative growth.

*34.0*  Scallop-topped Sawtooth Mountain (elev. 10,262 ft.) at 12:00. The spires were created by ice wedging along joints in the rock.

*34.9*  Highway passes through weather-closure gates.

*35.3*  Long Lake on the right covers 80 acres and is one of the more popular alpine bodies of water in the Beartooth Mountains. Because of the high oxygen content and low bacteria action, the water is virtually pollution free. Its proximity to the highway lends to active fishing that requires frequent stocking of cutthroat, brook, and rainbow trout. A Wyoming fishing license is required—available at Top of the World store (milepoint 38.8).

The strip of land between the highway and the lakeshore was the site of a worker's camp (McNutt and Pyle, Inc.) during construction of the plateau part of the highway *(see Beartooth Construction, pp. 28-29)*.

*35.7*  Morrison jeep road (USDA Forest Service Road 120) on left; access leads to Camp Sawtooth *(see History, pp. 12, 14)*.

*35.9*  Bridge across Long Lake outlet. The bridge is one of five remaining structures from the original Beartooth Highway. Built in 1934 by supplemental labor from the Civilian Conservation Corps (CCC), it illustrates the craftsmanship of hand-chiseled granite used in the abutments.

*36.7*  Little Bear Lake on right.

*37.0*  Small turnout on left at Chain Lakes viewpoint. The logic of terrain suggests that General Sheridan's expedition party passed down this valley on August 28, 1882 *(see Beartooth Expedition, pp. 16-17, 20)*.

*37.3*  USDA Forest Service Road 149 on left leads to Sawtooth Lake.

*Top of the World store at its original location at Beartooth Lake, circa 1938.* FLASHMORE COLLECTION

| Miles | Description |
|---|---|
| *37.4* | Excellent view of Beartooth Butte (elev. 10,514 ft.) at 12:00. This upland is one of the largest remnants of sedimentary rock layers on the uplifted granite surface of the mountains *(see Geology, p. 2)*. |
| *37.5* | Pilot Peak (left) and Index Peak on distant horizon at 11:30. |
| *37.6* | Island Lake Campground road to the right—one of the more popular recreational sites in the Beartooths. |
| *38.2* | Bridge across Little Bear Creek. |
| *38.8* | Top of the World store on right was originally located at Beartooth Lake. The store was built by Frank Marino in 1934 and did a thriving business during construction of the Beartooth Highway. It was moved to its present location in 1966. |

*A pretty good day at Beartooth Lake, circa 1930.* FLASHMORE COLLECTION

| Miles | Description |
|-------|-------------|
| *39.0* | Route recrosses Little Bear Creek. At this location, the creek cascades through a scenic gorge (right) that ultimately empties into Beartooth Lake. |
| *40.2* | Fire lookout tower (through trees at 12:00) is located on top of Clay Butte (elev. 9,811 ft.). |
| *40.7* | **Recommended Stop 4:** Road on right to Beartooth Lake and campground affords scenic views of the lake and Beartooth Butte. The Beartooth Expedition, led by General Philip H. Sheridan, camped on the north (opposite) side of the butte on August 27, 1882. He referred to the highland as "Red butte" *(see Beartooth Expedition, pp. 16, 20)*. |
|  | Near an early-day forest ranger cabin, a facility called Camp Beartooth (now razed) was located along the east shore where the present campground now exists. An isolated encampment, it catered to a hardy clientele mainly in the early years. A lodge, constructed in 1933 by Roy Hicox, |

quickly gained a reputation as a pristine, sought-after resort. Following completion of the Beartooth Highway in 1936, the remote gathering place became extremely popular for good food and for its outdoor summer dances along the lakeshore. Frank Marino's store was added nearby in 1934. Improvements to the resort in 1940 by Herb Flatt included a larger lodge and nineteen log cabins. In 1951, the facility was purchased by John and Mildred Griffin, who added a gift shop, a boathouse, and a bathhouse. They changed the name to Beartooth Lake Lodge and Resort, and advertised the place as "a dude ranch with city accommodations." By the early 1960s, however, pickup and trailer camping caused the business to dwindle, and in 1966 the Forest Service lease was not renewed.

Shortly thereafter, most of the buildings were torn down and others were sold to area residents. The store, now at Top of the World (milepoint 38.8), is all that remains of this once vacation utopia.

**CCC Bridges**

*Long Lake outlet, milepoint 35.9*

*Little Bear Creek, milepoint 38.2*

*Little Bear Creek, milepoint 39.0*

*Beartooth Creek, milepoint 40.9*

*Lake Creek, milepoint 48.6*

*40.9*     Bridge across Beartooth Creek (lake outlet).

*41.1*     Small turnout (very small) on right is used for viewing scenic Beartooth Falls on left.

*41.5*     Turnout on left **(caution)** for view of scenic Beartooth Creek Canyon. The creek empties into the Clarks Fork (middle distance) approximately 8 miles beyond.

*42.2*     **Recommended Stop 5:** Clay Butte road to right. This 3-mile (one way) side trip to the fire lookout tower provides magnificent views of Beartooth Butte,

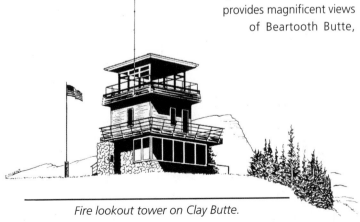

*Fire lookout tower on Clay Butte.*

*Ernest Hemingway cabin at the old L Bar T Ranch.*

| Miles | Description |
| --- | --- |

the Beartooth Mountains, the Clarks Fork valley, and the high peaks of the Absaroka Range, which form the east boundary of Yellowstone National Park. The facility ended its official service in 1975, but is usually staffed by volunteers during the summer months. Visitors are welcome to view fire-management exhibits, memorabilia, and historical and environmental interpretations. The high-country meadows that surround Clay Butte provide a profuse variety of summer wildflowers.

**42.3** Begin gradual descent of west side of the Beartooth Plateau toward the Clarks Fork valley.

**43.0** **Recommended Stop 6:** Turnout on left provides a scenic view of the Clarks Fork valley at the confluence of the Clarks Fork and Crandall Creek (10:00). The creek provided an escape route for the fleeing Nez Perce tribe in 1877 (see milepoint 60.3).

*43.2*   **Recommended Stop 7:** Pilot–Index overlook on right provides an excellent view of the upper Clarks Fork valley, backdropped on the west by high peaks of the Absaroka Range. The 40-mile-long valley was formed by a large glacier that originated in the Beartooth high country to the north.

The impressive landscape panorama from this vantage point also includes Pilot Peak on the left (elev. 11,708 ft.) and Index Peak on the right (elev. 11,313 ft.). The reddish-hued peak on the distant horizon at 2:30 is Fisher Mountain (elev. 10,237 ft.). It is part of the mineralized area of the New World mining district northeast of Cooke City.

*43.5*   Highway maintenance yard on left. The deep soil cover on this flank of the plateau supports fertile groves of aspen, which provide colorful displays during the fall months.

*45.5*   Muddy Creek road (USDA Forest Service Road 136) on right.

*48.1*   **Recommended Stop 8:** Clarks Fork overlook turnout on left. The prominent gray cliff across the valley (known locally as "the Reef") is a bed of limestone that is traceable the entire length of the Clarks Fork valley.

The devastation scars of the 1988 Yellowstone fire, called the Clover-Mist burn at this location, are evident along the opposite lower slopes of the valley.

The buildings on the valley floor at 2:00 (near the mouth of Onemile Creek) are the original structures of the former L Bar T Ranch, one of the earliest guest retreats in the area. It was named for a previous owner, Lawrence Nordquist, using the first and last letters of his name. The place was a favorite hideaway of Ernest Hemingway. In the summer of 1930, the novelist worked here on his bullfighting story, "Death in the Afternoon," fished the Clarks Fork, hunted the Absarokas, and voiced concern that a rumored highway soon to be constructed across the Beartooths would surely drive all the game away. The high-country environs of the secluded ranch were a constant distraction to the writer's literary concentration. During one 3-day respite, he caught a total of 92 trout, and would later declare that the best fishing in the world was on the Clarks Fork.

*48.6*     **Recommended Stop 9:** Bridge across Lake Creek. The Lake Creek Wayside is represented by a retained segment of the old highway and bridge, which was bypassed by the newer bridge built in 1974. The original bridge is similar in construction to the other CCC-built crossings at Long Lake, Little Bear Creek, and the outlet of Beartooth Lake. The falls upstream cascade through a scenic narrow chasm and are worth the short hike.

*49.0*     Lilly Lake road (USDA Forest Service Road 130) to right.

*Dude ranch trail ride along the Clarks Fork valley, circa 1940.*
MONTANA HISTORICAL SOCIETY

## PART III  CLARKS FORK VALLEY

The Clarks Fork valley is dominated by the twin beacons of Pilot and Index peaks that appear to stand guard over this sometimes forgotten pathway of American history. Here along the course of the river valley passed annual hunting forays of Indians, and later, mountain men, trappers, explorers, prospectors, miners, teamsters, and soldiers. Settlement was slow in this virtually inaccessible and lonesome country, and not until a wagon road was constructed in 1885 from Cooke City to the flats below did ranching and other businesses develop.

The valley might also be called "dude ranch alley": ranches "raising" dudes probably outnumber those raising cattle. At least ten guest ranches are located in the vicinity. The "dude business" began shortly before the turn of the century and was born out of isolation, hospitality, and pure economics. Stockgrowers began taking in paying guests to help offset expenses, and in the process played a major role in attracting thousands of people to the West. Mary Rinehart, writing for *Saturday Evening Post* (1925), described four significant migrations to the American West—soldiers, miners, cowboys, and "dudes." Ultimately, the cottage industry prospered and rapidly developed into a unique American institution that contributed significantly to the financial base of the local area. During a high period of popularity in the 1930s, 95 dude ranches were counted in Wyoming and 114 in Montana.

The term "dude," now obsolete in referring to a Western vacation, implied inexperience and ineptness. "Guest ranch" or the more rugged "outfitters" is more acceptable these days, and connotes a greater sense of adventure and self-reliance. In recent years, some guest ranches along the Clarks Fork valley have hosted summer programs for ecological, geological, and environmental groups.

| | |
|---|---|
| *49.9* | **Junction;** Wyoming Highway 296 leads to Cody; **continue straight ahead**. The road to Cody (62 mi.) via the lower part of the Clarks Fork valley is also known as the Chief Joseph Highway. The scenery is exceptional, including such attractions as Cathedral Cliffs, the Clarks Fork Gorge, Sunlight Basin, and the bridge over Sunlight Creek Canyon—the highest span in Wyoming. The view from the summit of Dead Indian Hill is one of the great panoramas of the northern Rocky Mountains. |
| *51.0* | Cattleguard; Jim Smith Peak high on the left at 11:00 (elev. 10,313 ft.). |
| *51.2* | Small turnout on the left; entering flood plain of the Clarks Fork of the Yellowstone River. William Clark (Lewis and Clark Expedition) named the river for himself. His only view of it, however, was at its confluence with the Yellowstone River (near present-day Laurel, Montana) as he passed by it on July 24, 1806. |
| *51.6* | RDS Ranch on the right is one of three properties at the north end of the Clarks Fork valley that actually raise cattle. |
| *52.4* | Crazy Creek Campground ahead on the left. |
| *52.5* | **Recommended Stop 10:** Bridge across Crazy Creek, named for its zigzag course. Small wayside on right (before bridge) affords parking for short hike to picturesque cascades. |
| *54.5* | Bridge across the Clarks Fork at the mouth of Pilot Creek (left). |
| *54.8* | Road on the left leads to Pilot Creek trailhead parking. |
| *55.3* | Entering Willow Park. General Sheridan's expedition party camped in the vicinity of this meadow on August 26, 1882, naming it Camp Clark after one of his staff officers *(see Beartooth Expedition, p. 19)*. |
| *56.7* | Highway crosses a large rockfall that was displaced from an upper ridge to the left. |
| *57.0* | Highway crosses Fox Creek; dramatic view upstream of Pilot Peak to the left. |

*Crazy Creek Falls.* MONTANA HISTORICAL SOCIETY

| Miles | Description |
|-------|-------------|

**57.9**   Route crosses Index Creek.

**58.8**   Re-entering Montana (Park County); boundary of Gallatin National Forest.

**59.0**   Route crosses the edge of an extensive rockfall area. Another rockfall occurs further north (0.5 mi.) along the highway.

**59.9**   Colter Pass (elev. 8,066 ft.), sometimes referred to as Cooke Pass. The drainage divide separates south-flowing Clarks Fork waters from west-flowing Soda Butte Creek waters. The pass was named for John Colter, a member of the Lewis and Clark Expedition *(see History, p. 7).*

**60.2**   Road on the right leads to a scenic gorge of the Clarks Fork.

**60.3**   Chief Joseph Campground on the left is named for one of the leaders of the Nez Perce tribe who fled east across Yellowstone National Park

*Pilot Peak (left) and Index Peak from near Willow Park and milepoint 55.3.*
PHOTOGRAPH BY ANDRE WILSE, 1898, COURTESY MONTANA HISTORICAL SOCIETY

| Miles | Description |
|-------|-------------|

following the Battle of the Big Hole in the summer of 1877. The seven hundred non-treaty Indians did not ascend Soda Butte Creek, nor did they rampage through Cooke City burning buildings, as some writings suggest. Making every attempt in their flight to avoid unnecessary confrontations with settlements, they passed to the south and crossed the Absarokas near Hoodoo Basin at the head of Timber Creek. Descending by upper tributaries of Crandall Creek to the Clarks Fork, the Indians made their way out onto the plains. Their plans for escape into Canada ended 50 miles short of the border, however, when they ultimately surrendered following the six-day Battle of the Bearpaw (September 30–October, 5, 1877).

**60.4**  Clarks Fork trailhead parking on the right.

*Chief Joseph.* NATIONAL PARK SERVICE

**Miles**     **Description**

*60.8*     Entering hamlet of Cooke Pass; meadow ahead on the left is the headwaters of Soda Butte Creek. The creek is named for a small thermal feature located downstream in Yellowstone National Park.

*61.1*     Entering back burn area; the burn was purposely set during the Yellowstone fire of 1988 to save the communities of Cooke City and Silver Gate.

*61.7*     Entrance to Colter Campground on the right.

*61.8*     Lulu Pass road on the right ascends Fisher Creek and is the eastern access to a scenic 10-mile loop **(not maintained; 4-wheel drive required)** that returns to US 212 via the Daisy Pass road (milepoint 63.1). The route leads to the New World mining district, which comprises five separate gold-copper-silver deposits that are currently owned by Crown Butte Mines, Inc.

*Grasshopper Glacier.* PHOTOGRAPH BY ANDRE WILSE, 1898, COURTESY MONTANA HISTORICAL SOCIETY

| Miles | Description |
|---|---|

At Lulu Pass the views are exceptional in all directions and include Chimney Rock to the west and Granite Peak to the northeast—the highest point in Montana at 12,799 feet above sea level. Midway along Fisher Creek, a jeep trail provides access to Goose Lake (5 mi.). Three miles beyond (via a hiking trail) is Grasshopper Glacier. This interesting feature displays massive hordes of ice-entombed insects that were apparently brought down in midflight by a storm and became embedded in the ice. Each summer, as parts of the glacier melt, the remains of the insects are washed out from the edge of the ice. Carbon-dating of insect fragments by the U.S. Geological Survey has determined the event occurred approximately 300 years ago. The best description of this phenomenon is provided by Andres Wilse, who accompanied the Kimball Expedition in 1898 as a photographer. Wilse relates the following:

> *We were told by hunters in slightly mystical undertones that far up in the mountains there was a mountain with a glacier full of grasshoppers. We didn't attach much value to this story, but one day I climbed up to the top of a 12,000-foot mountain in order to take measurements of the direction of a water course. I had completed my observations when I looked down at the foot of the mountain. Here I saw a remarkable sight. It was a glacier—but one with a surface which looked like the skin of an elephant. I went down to it and found that the stripes that went sideways across it were piles of dead grasshoppers. At the foot of the glacier there were railroad car-sized loads of shells, bodies, and legs of grasshoppers. In the crevasses of the glacier I could see thick layers of these insects. Far down in the crevasse I could see one layer of grass-hoppers and one of ice, and then grasshoppers again. I filled my flask with samples and I tell you there was a stir in camp when I came back and described my discovery! (Courtesy: America & World Geographic Publishing).*

*Early-day Cooke City—high, wide, and lonesome!*

62.9    Entrance to Soda Butte Campground on the left. Historic Cooke City cemetery, a short distance beyond, holds the remains of those who dreamed of glory strikes, including one of the town's founders, Adam (Horn) Miller.

63.1    Daisy Pass road on the right. Daisy Pass (5 mi.), via Miller Creek, affords a scenic panorama of the headwaters of the Stillwater River (north), and of Index Peak, Pilot Peak, and Republic Mountain (south).

63.2    Republic Mountain (elev. 10,170 ft.) at 11:00.

64.0    Entering Cooke City (elev. 7,651 ft.), situated along Soda Butte Creek at its confluence with Republic Creek. The town was originally named Shoofly by Adam (Horn) Miller, who, in 1869, along with three cohorts, made the initial placer-gold discovery. A year later, as news of the strike broke, other prospectors located claims on Republic Mountain and nearby Miller Mountain, and the New World mining district was born.

The ramshackle tent camp of Shoofly was renamed Cooke City in 1880 in honor of Jay Cooke Jr., an eastern financier of the Northern Pacific Railroad who had invested in mining property in the district. The motive for the name change was to encourage a rail line to the community to help develop mining interests. The eventual line was called the Cinnabar & Cooke, but the venture failed mainly because an environmentally conscious U.S. Congress refused to grant right-of-way easements through Yellowstone National Park. Cooke apparently never visited his namesake town.

*"With this place it's either boom or bust. Take your pick and good luck."*
*—Cooke City miner, 1948*

During its heyday (mid-1880s), Cooke City was a raucous place that by some bizarre formula estimated a population determined by the number of its saloons—13 at one point. This roughly translated to about 2,000 souls, assuming of course that they "all came to water." Today, Cooke City (an unincorporated town) enjoys a successful economy. Completion of the Beartooth Highway in 1936, which ultimately accessed a northeast gateway to Yellowstone National Park (4 mi.), provided the hamlet with a reasonably stable economic base from recreational revenues.

End of road log.

# RECREATION GUIDE

◆

USDA Forest Service campgrounds along the Beartooth Highway are open from June until the highway is closed by snow, usually in September. Some, at lower elevations near Red Lodge, stay open longer. Campsites are filled on a first-come, first-served basis. Trailers are permitted where noted, but there are no utility connections. A "unit" includes parking, tent spaces, table and benches, and a fire grate. Fees are required for most campgrounds. The stay limit is 10 days for Montana and 14 days for Wyoming.

## HOW TO BE BEAR AWARE

1. Never get close to bears.
2. Make noise while hiking.
3. Hike and explore in open areas.
4. Unleashed dogs and bears don't mix.
5. Keep your campsite clean; store food in closed containers.
6. Stay calm and quiet if you meet a bear; do not make sudden movements.
7. Report any bear activity.
8. Inquire at the nearest USDA Forest Service office for more information.

Bears are unique and beautiful animals that fascinate most people. People who recreate in bear country have a responsibility to understand bears and to minimize disturbances to them. As with most animals, gathering food and feeding are important, time-consuming activities. In the spring, bears are found at low elevations along streams or in open meadows where they feed on winter-killed animals and grasses. In summer, bears grub for roots and other plants on hillsides and in avalanche chutes, and occasionally feed on insects along talus slopes at the higher elevations. In fall, they often feed in huckleberry patches and whitebark pine stands.

Bears are most active early in the morning or late in the evening. They normally bed near cover in the middle of the day. Bears' tendency to be more active during low-light hours explains why few of us see them in the wild. Bears generally fear humans and will leave the area before we are even aware of their presence.

There are three situations in which people need to be particularly careful: (1) surprising bears at close range, (2) surprising bears while they are eating, and (3) surprising or approaching a female with cubs. Bears may be dangerous in these situations because they have a natural instinct to protect themselves, their food, and their young. Making bears aware of your presence and then avoiding them is your best protection.

# FOR ADDITIONAL INFORMATION

Custer National Forest
2602 First Ave., North
Billings, MT 59103
Phone: (406) 657-6361

Gallatin National Forest
3710 Sallon St. No. C
Bozeman, MT 59715
Phone: (406) 587-6701

Shoshone National Forest
808 Meadow Lane
Cody, WY 82414
Phone: (307) 527-6241

Beartooth Ranger District
Custer National Forest
Box 3420
Red Lodge, MT 59068
Phone: (406) 446-2103

*Springtime touring on the Beartooth Highway,* circa *1939.*
MONTANA HISTORICAL SOCIETY

# SUGGESTED READING

◆

Alt, David, and Donald W. Hyndman. *Roadside Geology of Montana*. Missoula, Mont.: Mountain Press Publishing Co., 1986.

Anderson, Bob. *Beartooth Country : Montana's Absaroka and Beartooth Mountains*. Montana Geographic Series, No. 7. Helena, Mont.: Montana Magazine, Inc., 1984.

Baker, Carlos. *Ernest Hemingway—A Life Story*. New York: Charles Scribner's Sons, 1969.

Beal, Merrill D. *I Will Fight No More Forever: Chief Joseph and the Nez Perce War*. Seattle: University of Washington Press, 1963.

Cheney, Roberta Carkeek. *Names on the Face of Montana*. Missoula, Mont.: Mountain Press Publishing Co., 1983.

Harris, Burton. *John Colter: His Years in the Rockies*. Lincoln and London: University of Nebraska Press, 1952.

James, H. L. *Geologic and Historic Guide to the Beartooth Highway, Montana and Wyoming.* Butte, Mont.: Montana Bureau of Mines and Geology Special Publication 110, 1995.

Janetski, Joel C. *The Indians of Yellowstone Park.* Salt Lake City: University of Utah Press, 1987.

Lovering, Thomas S. *The New World or Cooke City Mining District, Park County, Montana.* U.S. Geological Survey Bulletin 811-A, 1929.

Mulloy, William. "A Prehistoric Campsite Near Red Lodge, Montana." *American Antiquity*, vol. #9, no. 2 (1943).

Whittlesey, Lee H. *Yellowstone Place Names.* Helena, Mont.: Montana Historical Society Press, 1988.

# INDEX

◆

# ABOUT THE AUTHOR

H. L. James is a former editor/geologist for the Montana Bureau of Mines in Butte. A native of New Mexico, he has authored historical and photographic books on Southwestern Indian subjects and history. He is an honorary life member of the New Mexico Geological Society, has served as president of the Montana Section of the American Institute of Professional Geologists, and currently serves on the Board of Directors of the Association of Earth Science Editors. He now lives in Seeley Lake, Montana.